CHASING *the* SILENCE

A CALL TO THE PLACE WHERE GOD SPEAKS

CHASING *the* SILENCE

A CALL TO THE PLACE WHERE GOD SPEAKS

BUKKIE ALLISON

Chasing the Silence
Copyright © 2021 by Bukkie Allison
Originally published by CredoFusion Books

Revised edition 2023

Published by
Sophos Books Ltd.
London
sophosbooks.com

For The River Course Ministries.

All scriptures quotations are from The Holy Bible, *New King James Version* of the Bible, Copyright © 1982 Thomas Nelson.
Scriptures marked:
KJV are from the *King James Version* of the Bible.
ERV are from the *Holy Bible: Easy-to-Read Version* Copyright © 2018 by Mission Assist.
NLT are from the *Holy Bible, New Living Translation*, Copyright © 1996, 2004, 2007, 2015 by Tyndale House Foundation.
NASB are from the New American Standard Bible, Copyright © 1960, 1971, 1977, 1995, 2020 by The Lockman Foundation.
ESV are from The Holy Bible, English Standard Version, Copyright © 2001 by Crossway.
NIV are from *The Holy Bible, New International Version*, Copyright © 1973, 1978, 1984, 2011 by Biblica Inc.
BSB are from the *Berean Study Bible*, Copyright © 2020 by Bible Hub.

ISBN 978-1-905669-35-6

All rights reserved. No part of this publication may be reproduced, stored in a retrieval system, or be transmitted in any form or by any means, mechanical, electronic, photocopying or otherwise without the prior consent of the publisher.

Cover illustration and design by Bukkie Allison
Photo by Marino Linic on Unsplash
Printed in the United Kingdom

CONTENTS

Dedication	7
Acknowledgements	9
Foreword	11
Hello!	13
Introduction	17
1. The Call	25
2. The Time	29
3. The Place	33
4. The Posture	37
5. The Protocol	51
6. The Agenda	55
7. The Reward	63
8. A Cloud of Witnesses	67
9. Secrets and Mysteries	77
10. Why Do We Have Unanswered Prayers?	85

For Bims.

ACKNOWLEDGEMENTS

I will like to express special appreciation to my scribal mentor and matriarch, Apostle Theresa Harvard Johnson, Scribal Commander of *The School of the Scribe*; thank you ma'am for your devotedness to us scribes and for your labour of love in providing us with priceless resources at *The School of the Scribe*, *The Scribal Conservatory* and *Scribal Prophets* group. Your teachings, guidance, and divine counsel released a grace that enabled me to discover my scribal realm and explore my calling as a scribe. Words are not enough to say how grateful I am for you. Thank you for all you do.

I am grateful to my pastors, Tayo and Monica Ladejo, who received me with open arms into their sheepfold; thank you for your steadfast love and your unwavering compassion towards me. *The Governing Church* community is home and your divine counsel to guide and to nurture has given me stability. I pray that God who sees all and knows all reward you both for your immeasurable worth to the body of Christ.

My sincere thanks goes to Tokunbo Emmanuel. Thank you for taking on this project; for reading it and commending the work, and for your counsel and guidance throughout the preparation of this revised edition. You are a gift to the scribal nation in Africa. May God, our Father, bless you for all you do.

FOREWORD

Chasing the Silence is more than a beautiful treatise on prayer. It goes behind the veil and reveals the powerful dynamics of intimacy with God – the interplay, intercourse, and interaction that occurs in the secret place, where God dwells. This is an invitation from God to a generation of God-seekers who desire more than the lethargic, uneventful, monotonic spiritual activity that popular religion often serves.

The effectiveness of prayer is not measured in decibels. Loudness is not a sign of authority. There is a time to raise the voice; there is also a time to be still and know that the Lord is good. Could it be that the shallowness of divine revelation in the church today is the result of our aversion to inner stillness? And as the author suggests, could this also be the root of unanswered prayer?

Bukkie Allison has written from the heart and from experience. She knows the Father who is in secret, and through this beautiful expression of her scribal grace, the Father is inviting us all to meet with Him on the top of the prayer mountain.

Chasing the Silence revived my appreciation of the "still small voice," and renewed my commitment to a life of obedience. May you, too, find grace to be willing and obedient, for this is a sure path to blessedness.

Tokunbo Emmanuel

Omega Word Outreach, UK

HELLO!

What does "Chasing the Silence" mean to you? I will begin by describing to you what it means to me. I see *The Silence* as a time zone that connects the natural and the supernatural. It is a borderline where I gain access to the other side. It is like the intersection of latitude and longitude lines that specify a location where something or somewhere might be found. *The Silence* is the place where my latitude and God's longitude collide; a place in the Spirit where, without fail, I can meet with God and have Him all to myself.

You may have noticed that I have a role to play. I seek God out. I go after His presence in the cool of day. I follow His footprints in the sand. I listen for the sound of His voice by the water brook. My lines of latitude go in pursuit of His lines of longitude until they intersect. It is pretty much like Moses climbing up Mount Sinai in answer to God's invitation. As Moses ascended the mountain, there came a time when he stopped climbing and fell on his face. At that moment, swallowed up by the cloud of glory, he knew that he had found God's presence.

From time immemorial, God has been calling us to intimacy. The call is out there, hovering in the cosmos. His voice lingers in our thoughts, in the sound of the winds of time. It is up to me to respond to the call, any time from the rising of the sun to the going down of the same. My heart pants after Him like the deer pants after the water brook. I shall rest only after I find Him.

Seek me whilst I may be found, He says. May the Lord never hide His face from us. It is a terrible place to be when the Lord's face is hidden. Oh, how I rejoice at the sound of running water, knowing that my Beloved is by the water brook wanting to soothe my parched soul. Sometimes it is the rustling sound that caresses the shrubs in the garden that tell me He is near. He will soon appear for our walk in the cool of the day. Such is the experience of seeking God when He may be found. As I seek, I will surely find, because He promised, "If you seek Me, you will find Me when you seek Me with all your heart."

The Silence is the twilight when nature starts to wind down from the hustle of daylight. It is the midnight when men slumber, priests keep watch, and shadows slither about like creepers. It is the breaking dawn when nature stirs, a new day is birthed, and the morning wakes. *The Silence* for me are these moments of undivided attention offered up as a solemn sacrifice to the One who is eternally deserving of *my* silence. Let Him rise. Let Him speak. Yes, speak Lord, for thy servant listens.

So, what does *The Silence* mean to you?

Prayer is a powerful gift, a grace made available for us to connect with heaven and negotiate events on earth. Men ought always to pray and not to faint. However, we must not forget this aspect of prayer for it is just as potent and powerful. It is a kind of prayer that does not require words. I call it *The Silence*. It is a place of communion where we go to listen and not babble. It is a place where we go alone and not in clusters. It is not corporate prayer. It is solitary confinement, where you are a captive of grace. It is you alone with God. It is a solemn, quiet exchange where the sole agenda is to hear Him. I call it *The Silence*.

When I find myself at crossroads, when the arm of flesh fails like it is designed to, when I am broken, I go in pursuit of *The Silence*. In the place, God speaks while I sit in the quiet. There He shows me His glory and writes His commands upon my heart. He repairs me and puts me back together again, piece by piece. He brings out the blueprint and the roadmap. He shows me where I am and where I need to be. He tells me what I need to do to make progress. He speaks, and I listen. *The Silence* resets and restores me. *The Silence*... the type of prayer where all I do is listen.

I ask again, what does *The Silence* mean to you?

I'm desperate for You... I'm lost without You. There is a way that seems right unto man, but the end thereof is destruction. How can you ascertain the way to go without *The Silence*? James admonishes us not to speak proudly about how we will travel and make a sale and make huge profits but that we should rather say, By the grace of God we will do this and that. What worked for the other may not work for you. If there are no two fingerprints alike, why do we suppose that there are duplicate plans and purposes of God out there? Why do we attempt to copy and compare ourselves with others when God said, "I know the plans I have for you, thoughts of good and not evil and plans to give you a hope and a future"? You can obtain the nitty-gritty of God's plan and purposes for your life... from *The Silence,* the place where God speaks, and you listen.

Selāh.

INTRODUCTION

To Moses, Sinai was the place of revelation. It represents a location where God revealed Himself to him. Moses had two major appointments with the Lord on this mountain, which can serve as patterns and symbols for us in our mountaintop communion with God. Surely, biblical accounts serve as examples for us to learn from.

God is calling us to ascend the mountain of intimacy. The mountain is a location in the Spirit where God calls us to come up hither. The song writer said, Zion is calling me to higher place of praise. The first pattern we see is that whenever God calls, He is calling us up to a higher place. He calls us to a place of elevation away from the mundane routine of our lives, from the drama of everyday brouhaha. God called Moses away from the people into a solitary place where the mundane activities of daily living could not disturb. We see this also whenever Moses went into the tent of meeting, outside of the camp where the tent was located. In this solitary place, the cloud descended and engulfed the tent and God spoke to Moses as one spoke to a friend. When was the last time you went on a retreat just so you could have God all by yourself?

The mountain is a location in the Spirit where God seeks to meet with us. Let's make a quick distinction between these patterns and symbols represented by Moses' Sinai experience.

Symbols

The mountain symbolises that high place where God calls us up to meet with Him, away from the distractions of everyday life. It is a solitary place where you go alone to meet with God. When Jesus was nearing His death, even though He had been accompanied by Peter, James, and John into Gethsemane, Scripture tells us that He later asked the three with Him to wait while He went to pray. We must have moments in our lives where we go up to meet with God unaccompanied. I ask again, "When will you go on that much-needed retreat just to be alone with Abba?"

The mountain also symbolises consecration,

where we go to bare our heart before the Father so we can receive what He has to say to us (Exodus 34:2). Be ready in the morning to climb up the mountain and present yourself to God.

Above all, Mount Sinai symbolises a place of silence; a place of quiet submission, where we go to listen and receive rather than to speak and make requests. This right here is the crux of this book (we will talk more about this in Chapter 6).

Patterns

Considering Moses' ascension to Sinai, we see a pattern where God calls a man (or woman) to the place where He is, which is above. God will always seek to elevate and not debase us. Each time God called a person in Scripture, they immediately transitioned from an ordinary status to a place of honour.

God calls us to come alone. He told Moses, No one will be allowed to come with you. No one should even be seen anywhere on the mountain. Even your herds of animals or flocks of sheep will not be allowed to eat grass at the bottom of the mountain. God expects us to seek His presence as individuals. As the deer pants after the waters so does my heart pant after you. The pursuit of God must be a solitary pursuit. Moses went up the mountain alone. You must seek to have God all by yourself.

When we go to meet with God, we must first understand that we are responding to His call. He called the meeting so why be in a hurry to speak? Mount Sinai showed repeatedly how the Lord God had much to say when Moses appeared before Him. It was a place where Moses received instructions and directives for the people he led, directives for the rest of their days. These instructions became the laws by which their lives where governed.

Likewise, on the mountaintop, that location in the Spirit, we receive instructions and directives that would govern our lives forever. What God gives to one would differ from what He gives to the other. (We will talk more about this in Chapter 9).

Moses' First Trek Up the Mountain

In Exodus 19, the children of Israel arrived the wilderness and camped in front of the mountain. On the third day, the Lord descended upon Mount Sinai with fire, thunder, and lightening, intending to speak directly to the people. He gave them the Ten Commandments, instructions about idols, altars, slaves, personal property, social responsibility, justice, sabbath laws, etc. The Lord spoke extensively about how He expects the children of Israel to behave when different scenarios present themselves. In other words, God gave the new nation a code of conduct. Unfortunately, the people responded to the presence of God with fear and opted for Moses to be the intermediary between them and God.

In Exodus 24, God invited Moses, Aaron, Nadab and Abihu, and the seventy elders of Israel to ascend the mountain where they saw God and feasted with Him. After the feast, God instructed Moses, in verse 12, to *"Come up to me on the mountain and stay here, and I will give you the tablets of stone with the law and the commandments I have written for their instruction."* Before Moses left for the top of the mountain, he appointed Aaron and Hur as judges for the people in his absence. Although Moses set out with Joshua to the mountain, Joshua waited at the foot of the mountain while Moses proceeded to the top and disappeared into the cloud of glory that covered it. Moses stayed there for forty days and forty nights.

The length of time Moses stayed on the mountain with God is significant in this story (we will touch on this in Chapter 6). As we examine what happened during those forty days, we will begin to appreciate the account much more and see our communion with God in a new light.

Moses returned to the people with the two tablets of stone inscribed upon by the finger of God, only to find that the children of Israel had built a golden calf and had begun to worship it in revelry, committing all kinds of atrocities. In anger, Moses shattered the two tablets of stone which the Lord had given him for the people. It then became necessary for the Lord to summon Moses a second time, so He could write His words on another set of stone tablets.

> *Then the Lord said to Moses, "Make two more stone tablets like the first two that were broken. I will write the same words on these stones that were written on the first two stones. Be ready tomorrow morning and come up on mount Sinai. Stand before me there on the top of the mountain. No one will be allowed to come with you. No one should even be seen anywhere on the mountain. Even your herds of animals or flocks of sheep will not be allowed to eat grass at the bottom of the mountain."* **Exodus 34:1-3 ERV**

This verse of Scripture is loaded. We will, therefore, take it in small bites and see what the Lord has to say to us. There are seven different parts of this verse of Scripture that we will explore in the following chapters. They are:

The Call

The Time

The Place

The Posture

The Protocol

The Agenda

The Reward

May the Lord grant us understanding of what He is requiring of us.

1

The Call

The call of God elevates man unto a high ground. It brings us into deeper things in Him. God calls us unto intimacy with Him, a communion much deeper than we are accustomed to. God seeks to converse with us as a man speaks with his friend. He spoke in this way with Abraham, Moses, and David.

Intimacy builds trusts and assures God that He can depend on us. It is a calling unto higher ground because He seeks to show us how we must live and how we can enjoy the victory that was bought for us on the cross. God desires for us to be engulfed in His light, understand the truth, and embrace His ways.

While the children of Israel were content with just knowing the works of God in diverse miracles,

Moses understood the ways of God. Knowledge of God's ways comes from a close walk with Him. There is a level of knowing that comes to us when we encounter God beyond what we can get from Him. We must understand that there is a call that requires us to draw nearer to God and makes us inquisitive about who He is and what He is about. It was this type of inquisitiveness that compelled Moses to draw near to the burning bush. Our hearts must be perpetually dissatisfied with the mundane if we are going to experience God in supernatural measures.

There is a burning bush around the corner, but you cannot see it if your heart is not inclined to seek God beyond what you already know of Him. I want to challenge you to seek God because what we already know of Him is shallow ground. The call to ascend the mountain is an invitation to a higher ground. Come up hither! It is an elevation. It is a promotion. It is a lifting. God wants to show you mysteries and secrets.

Did He not say that He will give you the hidden treasures, and the riches stored in secret places? When a person proposes to give you something that is supposedly hidden from others, your first inclination would be to feel indebted to the person. You would wonder what favour they might want in return. When they manage to fulfil their end of the bargain, you are likely going to want to pledge your allegiance to them. If a mere man would require from you a level of commitment and loyalty before he shows you secret things, how much more God who made us in His likeness?

If your present level of communion with God is yet to uncover treasures, you perhaps need to draw nearer to Him. Leave the small matters behind and begin your climb up the mountain. Leave the haggle of the marketplace behind with those content with selling the truth for lesser gains and begin your solitary trek up the mountain. Decide today to answer that call, 'Come up hither!' Make an appointment with Abba for He has much to say to you. Come up hither! Come up here, come up now! The Most High beckons to us to draw closer to Him and to unfasten ourselves from the weights that keep us on ground level.

> *And the Lord called Moses to the top of the mountain.* **Exodus 19:20**

THE CALL TO COME UP HIGHER

Samuel was only a child when God's call came to him. The call elevated him from being a mere child to becoming God's oracle. Indeed, God's call is a call of elevation, transformation, and lifting. It draws us nearer to God and to His voice. When God calls us to come up hither, He intends to speak to us, and we must be prepared to listen.

Through His words and instructions, God lifts and transforms us.

When Joshua rose to lead the children of Israel, he was no longer the young captain who followed Moses from place to place. He was different now. He had become a general. But his transformation did not happen overnight. Joshua had become accustomed to seeking God in the secret place. Whenever Moses left the tent of meeting, Joshua would linger behind, perhaps so the cloud of glory may rub off on him or he could hear the voice of God. Joshua, under Moses' mentorship, had developed the keen pursuit of God's voice beyond the mundane.

As you respond to the call of God, you too will experience a transformation in your life.

2

The Time

As priests of God, we should be waking up to Him when the world is falling asleep. We should be able to shut out the noise and lock in *The Silence*. I cannot overemphasise the essence and importance of rising early for the sole purpose of meeting the Lord without distraction. This is the secret place, and it is God's desire that we come to Him each morning; meet with Him in at the top of the mountain.

> *I love them that love me; and those that seek me early shall find me.* **Proverbs 8:17 KJV**

There is a time to appear before the Lord; when creation snoozes in the still of the night; when men slumber and evil scurries about, hiding its face in the shadows; when the sun is below the horizon. We are most awake at this time; our eyes search the heavens, our hearts seek His voice, our lips mutter deep mysteries that our minds cannot comprehend. We are preparing to enter the garden, into the upper room. We are beginning our ascent up the holy mountain of God.

> *O God, thou art my God; early will I seek you, my soul thirsts for thee, my flesh longs for thee in a dry and thirsty land, where there is no water.* **Psalm 63:1 KJV**

David described his desperation for God in metaphors that suggest a negotiation between life and death. How desperate are you for God? The degree to which you desire Him will determine how early and how often you go in search of Him. He can be reached by those who call on Him. He will be found by those who seek Him. He is near to those who have regular communion with Him.

These are the ones who, like David, search for Him in solitary places. They know they do not have to search hard before they find Him; they do not have to reach too far to touch Him. They do not struggle to hear Him because they are aware of God's presence. They are the seekers of and perpetual cravers for His voice, His touch, His glory. I want to be one of such people. I want to be a seeker. I want to rise early and stand before Him way before the sun rises and kisses the sky.

3

The Place

The Lord bids us to come up the mountain, the location in the Spirit where Heart meets heart. This speaks of the presence and abode of God, where He might be found. The secret place.

The climb to the top of the mountain is a solitary journey, not a rat race. It is a decision made within the recess of one's heart. It is a deliberate pursuit of God. It is the pursuit of *The Silence*. It is not a noisy place. Rather, it is the journey up the mountain. It is Joshua sitting outside the tent of meeting and refusing to go away. It is Peter, James, and John seeking something deeper than the mundane. It is the woman at the well, asking for the water that never runs dry.

The Silence is a location in the Spirit. It is the top of the mountain, away from idol worship and the revelry of carefree living. It is a place where man goes boldly before His creator as mediator and bridge. A place where you say to God, "Choose me, make me worthy, send me." It is a place where we expect to encounter His glorious presence, the cloud of glory, the Shekinah of God. It is a place where you encounter the place of His habitation. where He dwells, where He settles. In this place, you long to meet Him face to face and hear Him speak with you as a friend. A place where friend makes convent with friend. A place of vows. A place of promises. A place of secret codes. A place of purple hues and the brilliant blue of lapis lazuli. It is a place we discover within time but is not calibrated by time.

Abba, you mutter with eyes wide open. Your heartbeat racing through the dark recesses of your mind seeking light. *Yahweh, show me your glory. Give me light. Give me understanding. Show me your glory. Give me light. Give me understanding.* Your words are few, but your longing is deep. Your craving is insatiable. Words fail you. But His Spirit comforts you.

You feel a fresh wind blow. You hear a whisper crack through the night. There is a rustle among the trees outside your window. Your heartbeat starts to slow down. A small breeze caresses your face. You see light break through the darkness. The burden lifts. Your knees bow down in worship. Your hands go up in devotion. He is here. Yahweh, the compassionate the merciful. He is here in the beauty of His holiness. Hallelujah!

4

The Posture

Why is it important that we come to God in a certain posture? Simply, because we want to get His attention. Both Cain and Abel offered up sacrifices to God. They both appeared before God with their offerings but only one of them had an acceptable posture.

We will learn the importance of posture from the story of Moses. God asked Moses to carve out two tablets of stone like the previous ones he shattered. God was going to write on them again (Exodus 34:1).

There is a limit to what men can teach you and it can only go so far. The fallibility of men will always get in the way of what is taught. In the end, we are mere men bearing these treasures in earthen vessels.

However, to complete the cycle of transformation in our lives, we must cultivate an intimate relationship with Abba in the secret place. After receiving instruction from men, we must eagerly go up the mountain on a treasure hunt and put ourselves in a position to receive the dābār of God in person.

Dābār, according to Strong's Lexicon, means speech, saying, utterance, word, words. When we enter the secret place, we receive the utterance of God from God Himself unto our spirit. We receive His spoken word. We hear His speech unravel inside of us like Moses heard it upon the mountain. This experience is limited when we are being taught by men. Teachings bring edification, encouragement, and sanctification.

This book, for example, is a form of teaching in written text. However, to encounter the voice of God that becomes one with your Spirit, you will have to go in pursuit of *The Silence*. Draw near to Him and He will draw near to you. Seek Him and He will be found by you. Go to the secret place and He will come to you. Go up the mountain with our tablets of stone and let Him write upon your heart even as He speaks to you.

A Call to Separation and Consecration

The spoken word of the LORD, whether it bears a blessing or a curse, is a flying scroll. It cannot take effect until we intermesh with it. If the voice of God is scarce in our day; if there is darkness and oblivion, it is because we are no longer listening, too busy talking, preoccupied with setting endless agendas, or consumed by our version of "ceaseless prayer." It is time we put away all distraction, consecrate our lives, and prepare to meet God in the secret place. This is a call to ascend the mountain.

God instructed Moses to consecrate the people and gather them at mount Sinai. Likewise, let us go with the expectation to hear Him! Amen! He will write His word into the fibre of our being. Let us become one with the word as ink becomes one with paper, as etching becomes one with stone. This is the eternal process that leads to true transformation.

> *The LORD came down in a cloud and stood there with him; and He called out His own name, Yahweh. The LORD passed in front of Moses, calling out, "Yahweh! The LORD! The God of compassion and mercy! I am slow to anger and filled with unfailing love and faithfulness. I lavish unfailing love and faithfulness. I lavish unfailing love to a thousand*

*generations. I forgive iniquity, rebellion, and sin. But I do not excuse the guilty. I lay the sins of the parents upon their children; the entire family is affected—even the children in the third and fourth generations." **Exodus 34:5-7 NLT***

Understand that the spoken word of the LORD that comes through revelation knowledge in the secret place is what, evidently, becomes the written word upon our hearts. When we come to God with a consecrated heart, like those two tablets of stone, we come prepared to receive the spoken word through revelation knowledge and in that receptiveness, the Holy Ghost writes His spoken word upon our hearts. He is thus able to bring the word to our remembrance because it is written upon our hearts. This is how we become one with the Word. This is how we receive the mark of the Master.

Moses immediately threw himself to the ground and worshipped. **Exodus 34:8 NLT**

When we encounter the spoken word of God through revelation knowledge, it immediately humbles us. Because through revelation, God reveals mysteries and secrets to us. This type of encounter only takes place in the secret place of *The Silence*.

The Heart vs the Tablets of Stone

When the Lord first spoke the Ten Commandments, the people trembled in fear. The Lord, therefore, called Moses up the mountain, gave him the laws upon tablets written by the finger of God, and sent Moses back to teach the people. After Moses shattered the tablets, God commanded Moses to come up the mountain again and bring two tablets of stone along so that He could write on them again.

I believe the Lord was demonstrating to us the proper way to listen to God; whenever God speaks, He is writing His words upon our hearts. And we should not reject His words like the Israelites did.

Just as God wrote His spoken word on tablets of stone for Moses to take back to the people, He also wants to write His words upon our hearts whenever He speaks to us. Hallelujah!

God wants us to bring our consecrated hearts to Him every morning in the secret place, so He may write and engrave His commands upon them. He also wants this be our daily routine. He is saying to us, like He said to Moses, "Come up in the morning unto the Mountain; bring your carved out stones that I may write upon them." The posture of heart here is our responsibility in the process. We bring our consecrated hearts to God and He, in turn, writes upon our hearts through the spoken word of

His grace. This word written upon our hearts is the word that bears witness within us. This is how we discern spirits and judge every teaching. God must first write His word upon our hearts.

> *So Moses chiseled out two tablets of stone like the first ones. Early in the morning he climbed Mount Sinai as the LORD had commanded him, and he carried the two stone tablets in his hands.* **Exodus 34:4 NLT**

The Lord detests idols. He detests it when we make graven images and worship them. Rather, He desires us to present our hearts as carved out stones upon which He could write His commands, daily. The only carved out "image" the Lord expects us to have fixed before our mind's eye is His word written upon our hearts, just like we do when we look into a mirror. In this way, wherever we turn, we always remember who we are in Him, who He has called us to be and what He has ordained us to do. Hallelujah!

The engraving process upon the heart of stone is symbolic of what Christ came to accomplish, which is to transform our stony hearts into hearts of flesh; where we become living epistles, just as He, Christ the Word, became flesh. The writing of the word (through Christ) upon our hearts is what produces a heart of flesh in us.

Being manifested that you are a letter of Christ, cared for by us, written not with ink but with the Spirit of the living God, not on tablets of stone but on tablets of human hearts. **2 Corinthians 3:3 NASB**

The true tablet of engraving is the heart. The tablets of stone were only a symbol. The heart of man is God's writing pad, God's engraving stone. This is where He writes either mercy or judgement.

In order to etch words unto stone, you will need to use a hammer and chisel. It involves a breaking process. When God writes His words unto our hearts, we must yield ourselves to be broken, to become malleable. We must yield ourselves to transformation.

"But this is the covenant which I will make with the house of Israel after those days," declares the Lord, "I will put My law within them and on their heart I will write it; and I will be their God, and they shall be My people. **Jeremiah 31:33 ESV**

"For this is the covenant that I will make with the house of Israel, After those days, says the Lord: I will put My laws into

their minds, And I will write them on their hearts. And I will be their God, And they shall be My people. **Hebrews 8:10**

Just as the engraved words become one with the stone, the word of God written on our heart becomes one with us. The word will either condemn or justify us because it is one with our conscience. It nudges and speaks to us and shows us the way we should go.

In that they show the work of the Law written in their hearts, their conscience bearing witness and their thoughts alternately accusing or else defending them... **Romans 2:15 NASB**

Write It Down Upon Your Heart

Then Moses carefully wrote down all the LORD's instructions. **Exodus 24:4 NLT**

This posture of heart places upon us not only a responsibility to continually inscribe God's word upon our heart, but also to document what we have received. At the second invitation up the mountain, there were two writing processes that took place.

> *Then the LORD said to Moses, "Write down all these instructions, for they represent the terms of the covenant I am making with you and with Israel." Moses remained there on the mountain with the LORD forty days and forty nights. In all that time he ate no bread and drank no water. And the LORD wrote the terms of the covenant - the Ten Commandments - on the stone tablets.* **Exodus 34:27-28 NLT**

First, God instructed Moses to come with carved out stones so that He could write on them. However, it wasn't just God who wrote, Moses also did some writing. He was instructed to 'write it down'. We need to present our consecrated hearts for God to write upon. We also have a responsibility to document what God says to us in the secret place.

In my book, *5 Ways to Steward the Anointing*, I wrote about this extensively. I described how we can be accountable in record-keeping. When we receive instructions, directives, inventions, and commands in the secret place, we must write them down; document them for archival purposes. Just like the Bible guides us through the scriptures, the things we receive in the secret place and write down will also serve to guide us through our journey. This is the very reason why we have the Bible today. The Bible was possible because scribes obeyed the instruction to "write it down!" and their many scrolls were collated into what we call the Bible today.

Another way the Holy Spirit administers our remembrance is by guiding us to things that we have written down. When we write the insights and instructions God gives us, we make a carved-out image of the spoken word and can behold it like a mirror every day. Through this, we never forget who we are in Him, what He expects of us, where we came from, and where we are heading.

Even scientists say that our capacity for retention is stronger when we write things down. The purpose of writing, in this context, is for retention. We can return to the written text later and refresh our minds with the words of God.

I cannot tell you how many times I have revisited journals I have written over the years and found direction for different phases of my life. Through these written thoughts, I have found light in dark tunnels, clarity in murky waters, and comfort in distress. It is such a powerful resource, and a prophetic one at that.

I cannot overemphasise the significance of God's instruction to "write it down". I can only urge you to develop the practice of journaling. Start writing down whatever the LORD, through the

Holy Spirit, says to you in the secret place, upon your bed, in dreams, in visions, in trances, through His prophets etc.

We should also write to preserve what God inspires in our heart that others may read and be equally inspired to run with perseverance the race set before them. This is why the Lord commanded the children of Israel to preserve the word of God through the generations and teach their children the commands of the Lord by writing it on the door posts, binding it around their necks and wrists, and telling it as stories to their children (Deuteronomy 6:6). Just as God spoke and Moses wrote the words down, Moses also taught the people the written commandments of God and urged them to write them on their doorposts. They, in turn, told it to their children who also wrote it upon their doorposts and bound it around their necks.

When God gave the tablets of stones, it was His way of demonstrating to us what He expects us to do with His commandments. He wants us to write them on the tablets of our hearts.

> *My son, keep my words, and lay up my commandments with thee. Keep my commandments and live; and my laws as the apple of thine eye. Bind them upon thine fingers, write them upon the tablets of thine heart.* **Proverbs 7:1-3 KJV**

We write what we have received from God upon our hearts by meditating upon the word; chewing the cud of the spoken and written word until we become one with it. So, be careful to listen for God's voice when He comes in those solitary moments. God, through His spoken word in your heart, is eager to give clarity and bring comfort to whatever may trouble you. Treasure your moments of meditation as the slow and steady inscription of God's dābār upon your receptive heart.

In Habakkuk, we learn about the power of writing God's word in our hearts. What we write becomes a propelling force that causes us to run the race of salvation. We also learn that the writer is the reader. The one who reads what was written and runs with it was also the one who did the writing. Until we write God's word upon our hearts, we cannot find grace to run the race with perseverance.

> *And the Lord answered me and said: "Write the vision and make it plain upon tablets, that he may run who reads it.*
> **Habakkuk 2:2**

What is Written is Eternal

When we write what God speaks, we create what He spoke. What was spoken becomes written and what is written is eternal. It becomes an image we can behold and believe. We become the word simply because we obeyed and inscribed it in our hearts.

That is FAITH.

We do not SEE IT,

But we BELIEVE IT,

Because IT IS WRITTEN in our hearts.

And we behold it just like we behold our reflection in a mirror.

Through the written word we see ourselves, and the word becomes flesh. As we go about our business, we do not forget! It is a continuous repeated writing where God inscribes upon our hearts and we, through mediation, continue to write His word upon the tablets of our heart.

In the beginning, God spoke, and His word became. Today, that spoken word is written upon our hearts by faith. Therefore, we speak that which is written, and by declaring it by faith, we create what was written. This is the creative process.

What is God speaking to you in the secret place about your today and your future? Write it down, meditate upon it, declare it by faith and through works, and by so doing you create it!

Spoken Word by God -> Written down and documented by us -> Written upon our hearts through meditation -> Spoken by Us -> Yields the Creative Process

In summary, a consecrated heart comes to God in the secret place for these four things to happen:

- For God to inscribe upon our hearts through the spoken word just like He inscribed upon the tablets of stone upon Mount Sinai. Here our hearts of stone become hearts of flesh; we become living epistles.

- We are persuaded to document what we have received in the secret place to preserve it, remember it, and teach it to others.

- We meditate upon the spoken word in order to soak in the dew of heaven that we have received, knowing that these meditative moments are the slow and steady inscription of God's word upon our hearts.

- The spoken word written upon our hearts yields the creative process that can perform what it says.

5

The Protocol

We have looked at the importance of rising early to be with the Lord and listen to what He wants to say. We have also seen the need to come with a consecrated heart and write the spoken word on our hearts through meditation. Now, we want to consider the need to prioritise this as a personal routine.

The call up the mountain is not the same as family devotion, where every member of the household is represented. Of course, these are important, but we must realise that God requires solitary time with us like He requested from Moses.

No one is to come with you or be seen anywhere on the mountain; not even the flocks and herds may graze in front of the mountain. **Exodus 34:3 NIV**

After God invited Moses up the mountain, Moses took Joshua, his assistant, along as he ascended the mountain. However, Joshua did not go to the mountain top with Moses. Instead, he waited for Moses and Moses continued up the mountain until he disappeared into the cloud of glory.

You meet God alone in the secret place. That is why it called the *secret place,* a place where you meet God *alone*. No besties accompanying you, no significant other, no mentees, just you and Abba. I love how A.W. Tozer put it: 'You must have God all by yourself.' God expects His sons and daughters to seek Him first, seek Him early, and seek Him alone.

Early will I seek you… **Psalm 63:1**

This prayer of David underscores the need for a solitary pursuit of God. At times, we are easily swayed by the crowd, by trends, and by viral media. We are scattered in different directions like sheep with no shepherd or sucked into the spotlight like fireflies. However, we need to disregard the demands of today's digital mob, turn a deaf ear to popular culture, give no attention to fashionable trends that demean godliness, and rather pay attention to the nudging of the Holy Ghost within us.

The Solitary Place

The solitary place, like the mountain of the Lord, is where the presence of the Lord dwells. It is a location in the Spirit where we receive visions of divine inspiration, inventions from the heart of God for his people, and instructions for our lives. It is a place for receiving detailed "How-tos" from God regarding different aspects of life. The question is, are we willing to ascend the top of the Mountain to receive these detailed instructions from the Lord? On the top of the mountain, we are to listen more than we speak. We come to hear God and not to hear ourselves. God does the speaking; we do the listening! We also write down what the Lord God says to us.

Prayer

Dear Father,

I want to thank You for the light that shines through whenever I read the written word.

I thank You also for understanding.

Thank You that we have understanding.

I see now that the place of Your GLORY, the SECRET PLACE;

that place upon the mountain is where we go to hear from You!

Oh Lord, You are more willing to speak to us than we are to You.

IF ONLY WE LISTEN!

We will hear wondrous things in Your presence!

Deepen our desire to hear you speak, and sharpen our hearing abilities.

Let our antennas be repaired and straightened to receive from You, oh Lord.

The mountaintop is a reception ground.

It is a place we go to HEAR not babble.

We HEAR and we WRITE!

6

The Agenda

God has more to say to us than we have to say to Him. He is eager to show us wondrous things that eyes have not seen nor ears heard.

In Exodus 20, the Lord gave the Ten commandments in the hearing of all Israel, but the people pleaded with Moses that they cannot bear to hear the Lord speak to them. The Lord, therefore, continued to give the laws to Moses. When Moses relayed the word of the Lord to the congregation, the people replied to Moses and said, "All that the Lord has spoken we will do." It was after these events that the Lord invited Moses up the mountain, the first invitation. Moses left Aaron and Hur in charge of the people and ascended the mountain to meet with God.

> *Then Moses disappeared into the cloud as he climbed higher up the mountain. He remained on the mountain forty days and forty nights.* **Exodus 24:18 NLT**

For the next seven chapters of the Book of Exodus, the Lord spoke to Moses and gave him instructions, design descriptions, and specifications about some vital things, including:

- The Golden Lamp Stand.
- The Tabernacle.
- The Altar of Burnt Offering.
- The Ark of the Covenant.
- The Court of the Tabernacle.
- The Altar of Incense and the Bronze Lava.
- The Anointing Oil (its preparations and all its ingredients).
- How to care for the Lamp Stand.
- Garments for the Priesthood.
- The Ephod.
- The priesthood of Aaron, Nadab and Abihu.
- The Daily Offerings.
- Specifications for the artisans, Bezalel and Oholiab, who would build the Tabernacle.

The Agenda

God communicated all these elements and their details to Moses on the mountain. God set the agenda, a clear and specific agenda, for Moses. He had much to tell Moses about the people he was called to lead. Sadly, many adopt scheming and cajoling for ministry and church growth tactics because they have neglected the secret place where God sets agendas and gives instructions.

Of course, the secret place is not for ministers alone. It is for every man and woman who seeks to live a fulfilled life. We must go to God to receive His agenda for our lives. Indeed, He has much to say to us.

Moses was on the mountain for forty days and forty nights, not to say prayers as we know it, but to hear God. He came out of this extended mountaintop prayer session with seven chapters of detailed instructions. Imagine what we might have missed during our quiet moments with God because we chose to babble instead of listen! Imagine the mysteries that God is eager to courier to us in the secret place!

Whenever we go before God in the secret place, we must realise that He has an agenda that towers far above any other matter we might bring before Him. God has an agenda! It may not be "seven chapters long" but be rest assured that He has an agenda for you. The question is, how long are we willing to wait on Him in silent meditation?

Noah and the Ark

The way Noah was described in Genesis 7 portrays a man who had an intimate relationship with God. Unlike many of us, Noah did not have the privilege of a church community where he was frequently inspired by gifted teachers. On the contrary, he lived during one of the darkest times of human history. In Noah's day, God looked at the atrocities of mankind and regretted that He had made man. Mankind was lost, yet Noah pleased God and found grace in the sight of God.

> *This is the account of Noah and his family. Noah was a righteous man, the only blameless person living on earth at the time, and he walked in close fellowship with God.* **Genesis 6:9 NLT**

Fellowship, as we know, is the communion of two or more people who have common interests. Noah spent time with God frequently and they both enjoyed fellowship like friends. I imagine that God will come to Noah like He visited Adam and Eve in the garden. I imagine that Noah would go to solitary places by the water brooks or a wide expanse of land, or even up a hill to worship. If Noah truly walked in close fellowship with God, then it is not a surprise that He would undertake such a daunting task as building the ark. Although, one would marvel at the several instructions that came with achieving this mammoth project.

I can picture Noah on his knees, worshipping God as usual. In comes Yahweh with His specific agenda. This is not the time for Noah to roll out a list of prayer requests. Rather, Noah needs to be silent before his maker because Yahweh has an agenda for this meeting.

> *And God said to Noah, I have determined to make an end of all flesh, for the earth is filled with violence through them. Behold, I will destroy them with the earth. Make yourself an ark of gopher wood. Make rooms in the ark, and cover it inside and out with pitch. This is how you are to make it.* **Genesis 6:13-15 ESV**

The most profound statement for me in this account is: 'And this is how you should make it.' Is it not amazing that God can come to man, a mere man, and give Him detailed, intricate instructions about something He wants man to do? It is my desire that God will come to me and say, "Bukkie, this is what I am about to do. I will like you to make something for me and this is how you should make it." It speaks of a trusted friendship with a dependable person. I want to be that person God can depend upon. When God says to his hosts,

'Who shall we send?' I want to be top of His mind as one He can trust.

As Noah listened, God started to give him measurements, specifications, descriptions, and requirements that would keep the ark afloat in a great flood. He also told him how to select the animals that would accompany him into the boat along with instructions for storing up food for the voyage. Furthermore, He told Noah what should happen after the flood.

We can all develop a close relationship with God at the secret place and become the person that God can depend upon.

The Sound That Shakes the Heaven

The whisper on the wind
Breaks my inhibitions
And settles me within
The mystery, you're closer than I think
Your still small voice moving me again
I hang on to every word you say
I live to hear you say my name

Speak to me
Speak to me
I'm listening

Unlock my ears to hear your voice
I want to know what you think
I want to know what you say.

(*Speak to me* by Kari Jobe)

7

The Reward

There is a reward for being the friend of God, someone God can depend upon and trust. He rewards those who respond to His call and do His bidding.

With God, intimacy ranks above familiarity. Familiarity, they say, breeds contempt. Men will despise you the moment they presume that they know everything about you. They will trample upon your self-esteem and belittle you because you have become common to them and there is no mystery about you. This is not the way God operates. Fellowship and intimacy with Him only breed elevation. Your confidence will grow bigger every time you come into His presence. As you grow in confidence with each encounter, His trust in you deepens. God can thus say of you like He said of Abraham, "Can I hide anything from my friend and not tell him what I am about to do?"

SEEING EYES AND HEARING EARS

The reward for spending time with God is the rub-off of His supernatural presence. You leave with particles of His glorious whiteness upon your clothing. His perfume lingers on your skin, and your face is awash with misty luminescence. Your ears are sharpened like never before to know His voice and to distinguish it from that of a stranger. The eyes of your inner man are opened. The breath of God awakens your spirit. Your inner eyes and ears are alert to the sound from the four winds of the earth. How do you think new sounds are birthed upon the earth? They come from the secret place of *The Silence*.

THE SHINNING FACE OF MOSES

> *Now it was so, when Moses came down from Mount Sinai (and the two tablets of the Testimony were in Moses' hand when he came down from the mountain), that Moses did not know that the skin of his face shone while he talked with them.*
> ***Exodus 34:29***

After forty days and forty nights of just listening to God, Moses' face had a luminous glow. Indeed, a shining face is one of the end products of staying soaked in the presence of God. Remember, Moses did not talk to God endlessly. He listened to God and wrote down what he heard God say.

> *The Lord bless you and keep you; The Lord make His face shine upon you, And be gracious to you; The Lord lift up His countenance upon you, And give you peace.* **Numbers 6:24-26**

This statement, "The Lord cause His face to shine on you," implies that God does not shine on everyone. He causes His face to shine on those who seek His face. There are many instances of people asking God not to hide His face from them (Job 13:24, Psalm 27:9, 44:24, 69:17, 88:14, 102:2, 143:7).

The Scriptural blessing goes on to say, "the Lord lift His countenance on you," which is a picture of a father smiling on and taking pleasure in his child. When the Lord lifts His countenance upon us, He is looking on us for our good. God wants to bless us. He wants to protect us. He wants to make His face shine upon us and be gracious to us and give us peace. Is the Lord's face shining on you?

> *May God be gracious to us and bless us and make his face shine on us.* **Psalm 67:1 NIV**

It is a great privilege to be honoured with God's presence, to find Him when we seek Him, to hear Him when He speaks. It is the precious, precious grace of God that avails for us.

> *Blessed are those who know the joyful sound, who walk, O LORD, in the light of Your presence.* **Psalm 89:15 BSB**

> *Many ask, "Who can show us the good?" Shine the light of Your face upon us, O LORD.* **Psalm 4:6**

> *Make Your face shine on Your servant; save me by Your loving devotion.* **Psalm 31:16 BSB**

Today, as you make these verses of Scripture your prayer, may the Lord come to you in the place where you stand to seek Him. May He cause His face to shine upon you! Amen.

8

The Cloud of Witnesses

When we consider the lives of those who embraced *The Silence*, the cloud of witnesses around us, we see a pattern where God is calling us to come up higher and to draw nearer. What is even more profound is the uniqueness of each person's call, a uniqueness that stemmed from what God spoke to them in secret. What He instructed one differed from what He instructed the other. Moreover, the success of these men and women was determined by the degree to which they followed what He instructed them to do. The cloud of witnesses will, in the following sections, provoke us to chase *The Silence*.

Samuel at Shiloh

Remember the young Samuel? Why did he say, "Speak Lord for thy servant listeneth..."? It was because he heard the Lord's call.

> *And it came to pass at that time... that the Lord called Samuel... then Eli perceived that the Lord hath called the boy... Therefore Eli said to Samuel, "Go lie down; and it shall be if He calls you that you must say, 'Speak Lord, for Your servant hears.'" Now the Lord came and stood and called as at other times, "Samuel, Samuel!" And Samuel answered, "Speak, for Your servant hears."* **1 Samuel 2:2, 4, 8, 9-10**

At a very tender age, Samuel received the inscription of God's word about judgment upon the house of Eli. God called Samuel by name and spoke to Him. All Samuel needed to do was listen to God. Our individual victories through life will depend greatly upon these moments when we answer God's call to come up hither, seek His face in the secret place, and receive His instructions. There is a time to speak (to pray and make requests) and there is a time to be silent (for God to speak).

A time to be silent and a time to speak.
Ecclesiastes 3:7b NIV

Joshua, Israel's New General

When God came to Joshua after the death of Moses, He admonished him in secret and said, "Be bold and very courageous." Joshua, from the time he used to accompany Moses to the mountain, was already accustomed to meeting God. It was during his time alone with God that God assured him of victory and a successful season of government as Israel's leader.

> *I will give you every place where you set your foot, as I promised Moses. Your territory will extend from the desert to Lebanon, and from the great river, the Euphrates - all the Hittite country - to the Mediterranean Sea in the west. No one will be able to stand against you all the days of your life.* ***Joshua 1:3-5 NIV***

The success of Joshua's tenure as Israel's leader hinged upon the instructions God gave him. There is only so much we can do by way of requests. Our ultimate assurance comes from what God reveals to us in the secret place.

Jacob and the Ladder at Bethel

Another example is Jacob. On his way to Paddan Aram to meet his uncle Laban, Jacob stopped at Bethel where he had a vision. In his vision he saw:

"Angels ascending and descending upon a ladder whose top reached to heaven. And there at the top 'stood the Lord.'"

And He said: I am the LORD the God of your father Abraham and the God of Isaac. I will give you and your descendants, the land on which you are lying... I will bring you back to this land and I will not leave you until I have done what I have promised you."

Hallelujah!

Jacob was not praying, yet God appeared to him. Why? Because God is more interested in speaking to us than hearing us speak to Him. God will appear to us at the top of the mountain or, as it was in the case of Jacob, at Bethel, the place of the ladder, because He has something important to say to us.

God put us here for a purpose and He alone can reveal that purpose to us. If we are going to live successfully here on earth and do the will of our

Father, then we need Him to reveal His will in the place of meditative prayer.

DAVID, WORSHIPPER AND FRIEND OF GOD

If there was anyone accustomed to the secret place and *The Silence*, it would be David, the Shepherd boy. When he played the harp and sang solemn songs to God, he positioned his heart and ears to receive from the Lord. There were many instances in David's life that demonstrated the importance of listening to God.

When the Amalekites raided David's camp, David enquired of the Lord, and then the Lord spoke to him: Pursue them, you will surely overtake them, and you will recover all. I imagine that David's prayer was both spoken and meditative, which allowed him to hear the response God gave. Making room for *The Silence* in our prayer routine will greatly improve our intimacy with God.

DEBORAH AND BARAK

When Deborah said to Barak, 'Thus says the Lord…' where and when did she receive the message she passed on to Barak? How is it that some people seem to know the intimate dealings of God and others don't? I would like to imagine that Deborah, a prophet, had a custom of going up the mountain to hear what He would say to her. And on this fateful day, she had received a message for Barak.

> *She sent for Barak son of Abinoam from Kedesh in Naphtali and said to him, 'The Lord, the God of Israel, commands you: "Go, take with you ten thousand men of Naphtali and Zebulun and lead them up to Mount Tabor. I will lead Sisera, the commander of Jabin's army, with his chariots and his troops to the river Kishon and give him into your hands."'* **Judges 4:6-7 NIV**

The instruction was specific. God selected two of the twelve tribes of Israel to accompany Barak into battle. He also specified the location where they were to assemble, and the place where victory would be attained.

Elijah and the Years of Famine

There are phrases commonly used throughout scripture that suggest God's spoken word: "And it came to pass" or "Thus says the Lord…" God's prophets always seemed to have a message from God. They were either prophesying or witnessing their word come to pass. Has it ever occurred to us how this was possible? How did Elijah, for example, know to say with confidence that there would be no rain on the land for three years? How did he receive a subsequent word about an impending downpour? Elijah and others like him were people of the secret place. They understood that to be God's mouthpiece to the people, their ears must be tuned in to hear God's voice.

> *After a long time, in the third year, the word of the Lord came to Elijah: "Go and present yourself to Ahab, and I will send rain on the land."* **1 Kings 18:1 NIV**

In Elijah's story, we also see a balance in the way he communed with the Lord. Elijah would receive the instruction or command in the secret place, where God spoke to him as a friend, and after receiving the word, Elijah would pray it through until he saw the manifestation.

> *Elijah was as human as we are, and yet when he prayed earnestly that no rain would fall, none fell for three and a half years!* **James 5:17 NLT**

> *And Elijah said unto Ahab, Get thee up, eat and drink; for there is a sound of abundance of rain. So Ahab went up to eat and to drink. And Elijah went up to the top of Carmel; and he cast himself down upon the earth, and put his face between his knees, and said to his servant, Go up now, look toward the sea. And he went up, and looked, and said, There is nothing. And he said, Go again seven times. And it came to pass at the seventh time, that he said, Behold, there ariseth a little cloud out of the sea, like a man's hand. And he said, Go up, say unto Ahab, Prepare thy chariot, and get thee down that the rain stop thee not.* **1 Kings 18:41-44 KJV**

The word of God came to Elijah in the secret place that there would be rain. However, before the rain manifested, Elijah committed himself to prayer at mount Carmel. This is a beautiful description of how we must conduct our spiritual lives in prayer. In that solitary place where we hear God's instruction, counsel, or secret formulas to inventions, we need to also travail in ceaseless prayer for the manifestation of God's word. The effectual fervent prayer of the righteous avails much. This cycle will continue until the breakthrough comes. We also stay tuned to *The Silence* peradventure God has more to say to us.

When We Meet With God

God is calling you to ascend the mountain. The cloud of witness is urging you to chase *The Silence*. When we meet with God in the secret place, we experience a manifestation of Isaiah 65:24: Before you call, I will answer, while they are still speaking, I will hear. When we meet with God in the secret place, baring our hearts and longing for His voice, He unravels mysteries, solves age-long conflicts, and solves matters that were seemingly impossible.

9

Secrets and Mysteries

Sometime in December 2016, I had a hearing vision. Half awake, as I was meditating on a research material for a project I was working on at the time, I heard these words loud and clear: *The birth of a secret is the unveiling of ten thousand mysteries.* Indeed, some of the things you receive in the secret place are for your personal consumption and not for general application.

God will give you blueprints, procedures, techniques, and formulas that are tailored to your peculiar circumstances. If you were to share them with others, you will mislead them and create a pandemonium.

When you meet with Abba in the secret place, expect mysteries and secrets. And when He reveals them to you, treat them exactly as such; as secrets, something to be cherished, something to keep close to your heart. Then wait for understanding. Wait for wisdom to give you direction. Every secret is a seed bearing ten thousand mysteries. And each secret will continue to unravel its depth of mysteries unto those who nurture their relationship with Abba in the secret place. How many times have you dreamed dreams and seen visions that are yet to manifest? Don't you have questions? Don't you wish for them to come to pass? Stay a little longer next time. Dwell another day upon this mountain. Wait upon the Lord.

Jacob, The Stalks and the Mating Goats

Have you ever wondered what exactly happened at Paddan Aram? How God made Jacob seven times richer than Laban even though Laban had changed his wages twenty times? How did Jacob come about the wisdom that seemingly influenced the mating goats in a supernatural manner? Bizarre, isn't it?

As mysterious as it looks, this is what God can do to enable a man or woman to gain victory over their challenges in life. Laban was oppressing Jacob, his nephew, but Jacob found help in the secret place. God, through His angel, revealed to Jacob hidden treasures and riches stored in secret places. After the vision, Jacob created a masterclass on how to breed spotted rams and goats. If judged in the natural, people would say Jacob had gone nuts.

God will reveal formulas that are specific to your calling and season in the secret place. If you are discerning, you would keep these secrets close to your heart and simply obey. Some things are not meant to be told on the hilltops; they should remain secrets and mysteries. There are secrets that require you to chew the cud until the mysteries within them are revealed.

Imagine that you are faced with tempestuous challenges and have exhausted your energies in extensive prayer sessions (which is good by the way, for men ought always to pray and not to faint), but have you also engaged *The Silence*? Have you considered taking that solitary trek up the mountain to the place where God might be found? Have you gone to Him and say, like Samuel, 'Speak Lord for thy servant listens…'?

If your finances are in dire straits, the health of a loved one is deteriorating, or your career is at stake, and you desperately need an intervention, God can send you a secret formula that is specific to your season and journey. He can download into your heart a secret that requires only your faith and obedience. A secret not meant for public review or consumption.

Samson the Nazarite

The life of Samson is another demonstration of the proverb I received in that vision: *The birth of a secret is the unveiling of ten thousand mysteries.* Samson was like a demigod with uncommon strength. He killed a lion with his bare hands. He slaughtered a thousand men with the jawbone of a donkey. He uprooted the gates of a city and carried them on his shoulders all the way to Hebron. It is speculated that the distance between Gaza and Hebron was over nine miles.

Samson was also a Nazarite. Let us take a close look at the requirements for fulfilling the vow of a Nazarite: He shall separate himself from wine and similar drink; he shall drink neither vinegar made from wine nor vinegar made from similar drink; neither shall he drink any grape juice, nor eat fresh grapes or raisins. All the days of his separation he shall eat nothing that is produced by the grapevines, from the seed to skin. All the days of the vow of his separation no razor shall come upon his head; until the days are fulfilled for which he separated himself to the LORD, he shall be holy. Then he shall let the locks of the hair of his head grow. All the days that he separates himself to the LORD he shall not go near a dead body. He shall not make himself unclean even for his father or mother, for his brother to his sister, when they die, because his separation to God is upon his head. All the days of his separation he shall be holy to the LORD (Numbers 6:1-21).

A Nazarite is someone who takes a vow to abstain from certain things for a specified time during which they are consecrated unto God for a specific purpose. What made Samson unique from the regular Nazarite was that Samson was a Nazarite from birth, and he was required of the Lord to refrain from all of these for his entire life. His was a life-long consecration.

Samson's life was the unravelling of mysteries within a secret. The angel of the Lord appeared to Manoah's wife, told her she would have a son, and gave her specific instructions identical to the vow of the Nazarite. He said, "He will be dedicated to God in a special way. He will be a Nazarite. So, you must never cut his hair. He will be God's special person from before he is born. He will save the Israelites from the power of the Philistines" (Judges 13:3-5).

Samson was God's anointed. His superhuman strength was attributed to his consecration unto God which was given to his parents as a strict instruction before his birth. He had long hair and according to scripture, they hung in seven thick locks. Within those locks of hair was a deep mystery, supernatural instructions, and divine commandments stored away for a specific purpose — to deliver the Israelites from their oppressors.

These mysteries made Samson supernatural. It took Delilah many days of scheming to get Samson to divulge what was meant to remain secret.

> *Finally, Samson told Delilah everything. He said, "I have never had my hair cut. I was dedicated to God before I was born. If someone shaved my head, I would lose my strength. I would become as weak as any other man."* **Judges 16:17 ERV**

The mystery of Samson's strength was meant to remain hidden. When we carelessly divulge the secrets of heaven given to us in the secret place, we become immediately vulnerable to the entrapments of the enemy.

> *Delilah saw that Samson had told her his secret. She sent a message to the rulers of the Philistines. She said, "Come back again. Samson has told me everything." So the rulers of the Philistines came back and brought the money that they had promised to give her.* **Judges 16:18 ERV**

The secret place of *The Silence*, where we come to as we ascend the mountain, is a location where we intercept heaven's mysteries and supernatural secrets. What has the Lord told you in the secret place? Store it up in your heart and await its manifestation.

> *Keep your heart with all diligence for out of it are the issues of life.* **Proverbs 4:23 KJV**

What are you hearing in the secret place? Some things are a secret and a mystery!

10

Why Do We Have Unanswered Prayers?

How is it that Abraham could suddenly get up and leave his hometown to go to a place where God will show him? It was because Abraham had a relationship with God that was beyond religious ceremonies and routine. This level of spiritual intimacy is akin to the pattern God demonstrated in the beginning with Adam and Eve when He had daily communion with them in the garden of Eden.

Throughout Moses' lifetime, God spoke to him and gave him instructions. This highlights the truth that it is possible to have such intimacy with God. It also underscores the point that amidst all our intercessions, petitions, supplications, and warfare, we must also have *The Silence*, a time when we retreat into the secret place to receive from God and hear Him speak to us. Like Moses, we need to enter the tent of meeting and ascend the mountain of encounters.

God, through the help of the Holy Spirit, can tell us wondrous things about our lives and purpose, and help us navigate our journey upon the earth. The word of the Lord came to Mary and Joseph, for instance, announcing the arrival of the Messiah, instructing them about His life and purpose, warning them of dangers in the land of their sojourn, and leading them to safety until the child was born.

After praying for long hours and nights on end, we must take time to listen to God. We must seek His face for answers, next steps, and clarity. We must not get cumbered with too many programs, meetings, and activities, to the point where we cannot spare moments to hear what God is saying in the now.

We do not hear God because we are, perhaps, too preoccupied with our list of needs, lengthy prayers, and anxious activities. We do not prioritise solitary time with Him. And when we try, we allow anxiety to creep in and steal what could have been a moment of quiet communion, revelation, and wondrous encounter. Our relationship with God, in truth, should be more about hearing God speak than it is about us blabbing.

After praying fervently and earnestly, let us also make out time to seek Him in silence. What He says to us in the secret place would ultimately guide us into divine happenstances that become answers to our prayers. Sometimes, God will guide us into what we should pray about. At other times, He shows us what is to come or gives us clarity in matters that are puzzling. Many times, in the secret place, God comes to instruct us about our next steps. This is how we can enjoy a succession of answered prayers.

In the Book of Acts, there is a story that amplifies this truth. Two strangers, one a Jew and the other a gentile, had a vision from God telling them what they must do for a specific purpose. Cornelius, a devout man with a fervent prayer life, had a vision. In the vision, an angel told him that his prayers have been answered. However, for Cornelius' joy to be full, the angel had instructions for Cornelius. God would show Cornelius what he must do (Acts 10:3-6).

Peter had also been fasting and praying. While taking a nap, the angel of God appeared to Peter in a vision and told him about a man he had never met, and what he must do when he meets him. The angel also informed Peter that two visitors had come in that moment to take him to this certain man.

The lesson for us from this story is that after we have spent time fasting and praying, we must remain in that place of expectancy because God might want to give us some instructions. According to scripture, "You will hear a voice behind you saying, 'This is the way walk in it.'" Fasting and prayer prepares our hearts for communion with God.

Pray Without Ceasing vs. Hearing From God

Sometimes, when we take our issues to our spiritual leaders, they ask us, "Have you prayed about it?" When we answer in the affirmative, they go on to ask, "What did God say?" I guess many people do not like that part of the conversation! They would rather that their pastors tell them what God is saying!

It is true that the effectual fervent prayer of the righteous avails much, and we ought always to pray and not to faint. Nonetheless, as we have established in this book, prayer is a dialogue and not a monologue. So, the question is valid: "What did God say to you after prayer?" God is more eager to speak to us than we are to Him. He said, Before you call I will answer, while you are yet speaking I will hear. He knows what you need. He is not a wicked Father. Therefore, rather than ask for things, He said ask for the Holy Spirit, because He is the One who will show us secret things.

Howbeit when He, the Spirit of truth, is come, He will guide you into all truth: for He shall not speak of Himself; but whatsoever He shall hear, that shall He speak: and He will show you things to come.
John 16:13 KJV

There is a hidden desire for the mystique in all of us and it is coming from the fact that the mystique is a tangible part of our world and our existence. This is the reason why many are hypnotised by occult communities masquerading as churches. Those who have not cultivated their lives in the secret place are susceptible to this kind of deception. Those who have not honed their inner ears to hear the voice of God will fall for any performer who claims to hear God. If you do not train your inner eyes to see secret things, you will fall for any charlatan who claims he has seen a vision. In the last days, your old men shall dream dreams and your young men shall see visions and your sons and daughters shall prophesy (Joel 2:28). These apparent mystical abilities are given to us by the Holy Ghost to benefit. Again, they are for our benefit.

God is not unjust to leave us to the mercies of charismatic fraudsters and con men. He has given us the Holy Ghost and the Scriptures. There is a time to seek Him in silence. There is a time to come before Him without an agenda. There is a time to ruminate upon the word of God. There is a time to wait for His instruction. If you seek Him, you will find Him when you seek Him with all your heart. After you have prayed and fasted, wait to hear Him for He will surely come to those who wait.

Revive the Place of Devoted Study and Meditation

After his conversion, it said that Apostle Paul spent two to three years in Arabia to reflect and seek the face of God for his ministry. I find this quite thought-provoking, and compelling. If Paul was truly a member of the Sanhedrin, a highly revered scholar of the law, taught by Gamaliel, one of the best, then you can only imagine the state of confusion Paul found himself after the revelatory experience on the way to Damascus. He certainly needed a season of reflection. His encounter with Christ called for time away to a place such as the desert of Arabia. Moreover, two to three years is not too much time for reflection if one must unlearn an indoctrination that took decades to install. We must not underestimate the power God makes available to us when we reflect, meditate, and ruminate.

You must give considerable time to searching Scripture. It is not enough to just read scripture, you need to search. The Scriptures are like the ocean, full of all kinds of mysteries, revelation, and treasures. Therefore, you must go beyond just reading the Bible and become a treasure hunter. Search out the riches of God's glory for they are encapsulated in His word. Whatever your dilemma, you will find the answer in the word of God if you take the time to search it out. Whoever seeks, finds.

Three things must happen as you search Scripture:

- *Read* several verses and make comparison with other accounts, translations, commentaries etc.
- *Pause* to ruminate for a few minutes, or for an extended time, sometimes in stretches as you go through your day or week.
- *Hear God* through the Holy Spirit speak to you in the recess of your soul. Again, those who seek shall find.

I must quickly add here that every message or teaching you hear in church should and must always send you back to Scripture like the Bereans. Go and search it out to see if it is so. Meditation is a powerful practice. It is like a fishing net that draws from the realm of the supernatural. If you keep the net sunk in the waters of the Spirit long enough, you will have a great catch. Do not be too quick to retrieve your net if the earliest moments seem empty and barren. You must learn to tarry in His presence. So long as you keep your net in the deep, you will certainly receive.

Listen, the word of God is like the ocean. Within its darkest depths is a city submerged with all kinds of mysteries, revelations, and treasures. Meditation is one way of drawing out of that submerged city. Your expectation will determine the size of your fishing net. It will also make you keep the net in the deep for as long as necessary, until you receive something tangible and treasurable.

Make it a lifestyle. Become a seeker. Become a treasure hunter. Become a lover of God, one that is obsessing to read His texts and receive His calls. Become a bride indeed, one that yearns incessantly for the attention of the Groom.

When we have unanswered prayers, might it be that we have neglected the secret place? Could it be that we have allowed the embers of the mysterious to go cold? It is time to reawaken our inner man and go in search of God in the secret place. Plunge into the river of the Spirit and let it take you upstream. Let its tides ferry you back to the source. Let the currents empty you into the crystal sea of our God. Rise early and begin your trek up the mountain, to that place where He might be found.

Selāh.

Contact the Author

email
therivercourse@gmail.com

instagram
@the_rivercourse

facebook
www.facebook.com/bukkie.allison

Other Books by Bukkie

Ruth & Orpah

A Prayer for You

21 Psalms of Bukkie

Hear These Voices

The Secret Life of a City Girl

5 Ways to Protect the Anointing

5 Ways to Steward the Anointing

Bukkie Allison is a scribe dedicated to seeking out treasures in God's word and sharing them with believers around the world, for edification of the body until we all grow into maturity in Christ. She finds great joy in sharing her solemn journeys in God with others. Apart from writing instructional teachings, Bukkie is passionate about unearthing untold life-affirming stories and publishing them for posterity. She lives in Lagos, Nigeria, where she works as chief strategy officer for her indie publishing company.

www.ingramcontent.com/pod-product-compliance
Lightning Source LLC
Chambersburg PA
CBHW071310040426
42444CB00009B/1956